THE
BOOK
OF
KNOWING

THE BOOK OF KNOWING

Know How You Think, Change How You Feel

GWENDOLINE SMITH

Andrews McMeel
PUBLISHING®

CONTENTS

AUTHOR'S NOTE   vi

INTRODUCTION   viii

CHAPTER ONE:
Figuring things out AKA Philosophy 101   1

CHAPTER TWO:
It's all connected   9

CHAPTER THREE:
Simple as ABC   27

CHAPTER FOUR:
The part reality plays   31

CHAPTER FIVE:
Thought content   39

CHAPTER SIX:
How to recognize a thought virus   47

CHAPTER SEVEN:
What now? How does all this theory work for me?   107

CHAPTER EIGHT:
Skills from the cognitive tool kit   121

CHAPTER NINE:
More helpful stuff   143

CHAPTER TEN:
Which track would you choose?   161

CHAPTER ELEVEN:
Winding down   167

IN THE END   170

GREAT MINDS THAT I HAVE QUOTED   172

GLOSSARY   173

ABOUT THE AUTHOR   178

AUTHOR'S NOTE

Four years ago I started a blog on Tumblr, askdoctorknow.tumblr.com. The idea came from a wonderful woman and poet, Lang Leav. She asked me one evening what thoughts I had on how to deal with young adult females writing on her blog about self-harm.

I put my psychologist's hat on and gave her some direction. Lang said, "You should have a blog. There are so many young people out there in cyberspace looking for help." So that was when Doctor Know was conceived.

My blog continued to gain momentum, and in one morning I received 11,000 questions. It was like an avalanche of young people wanting to know which way to turn. I was overwhelmed.

It was wonderful, but difficult to get back to everyone needing help. One day a colleague said to me that Doctor Know seemed to have tapped into the main vein of unmet need in youth mental health services worldwide. I realized that I needed to construct another way of addressing the issues facing young people.

That was how this book, *The Book of Knowing*, came to be written.

— Gwendoline Smith (AKA Doctor Know), 2019
B.Soc.Sci., M.Soc.Sci. (Hons.), Dip.Clin.Psych.

INTRODUCTION

The Book of Knowing will teach you how to adapt and feel better about your place in the world.

Have you ever wondered why you don't seem to have any control over your feelings? How they can turn up and whack you in the back of the head when you thought you were having a reasonable sort of a day?

What about those times when you are just trying to blend in with a group and your face turns bright red—what's that about?

Or those times when you finally pluck up the courage to go and talk to your teacher or your boss, then your stomach fills with butterflies, you blush, your heart pounds so loud you can't hear yourself

think, and then you have to sit down because you feel like your legs have turned to jelly? Does this all sound familiar?

The Book of Knowing sets out to explain clearly what is happening to you in these situations. It helps you understand yourself better and learn ways to manage your feelings more effectively.

The Book of Knowing achieves this by educating you in a practical way about how you think. It is a book full of life skills. It is about learning the way of thinking that fosters resilience, which enables you to deal with many of the unnecessary anxieties that plague you.

This is not a book about illness. It does not encourage you to announce to the world, "Hey, look at me, I have **social anxiety**!" It is a book that says:

"I am learning about how I think and, as a result, how I feel."

The essence of *The Book of Knowing* is taken from the school of **cognitive behavioral therapy (CBT)**, founded by Dr. Aaron Beck. CBT is recognized as a highly effective, evidence-based therapeutic approach for the treatment of mood disorders, **depression**, **anxiety**, and general dissatisfaction with life.

Utilizing this method will help those of you with diagnosed conditions. It will also be both preventative and remedial for those of you who experience life as just too difficult.

The tone of *The Book of Knowing* is intended to be practical, educational, and informative, with humor and fabulous illustrations throughout. So I hope that you enjoy and learn and have a laugh.

CHAPTER ONE

FIGURING THINGS OUT AKA PHILOSOPHY 101

I never quite made it to the philosophy department in college. A psychology major allowed me more time to pursue my other passion—playing eight-ball.

In recent years, since studying cognitive behavioral psychology, I have become quite keen on a guy called Socrates. I would have to say he is my favorite philosopher. He was saying really interesting stuff way back in circa 470 BC. (Yes, long before the internet.)

He was committed to the concept of reason. He believed that, properly cultivated, reason can and should be the all-controlling factor in life. Not surprisingly, being such a pioneering and brilliant mind, he was sentenced to death by poisoning because of his refusal to acknowledge the gods recognized by the state and for his supposed "corruption of youth"—I would have referred to it as enlightenment!

Socrates was probably the most extraordinary

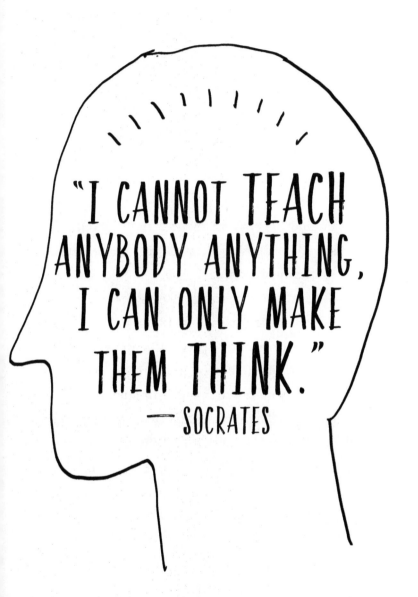

"I CANNOT TEACH ANYBODY ANYTHING, I CAN ONLY MAKE THEM THINK."

— SOCRATES

mind of the time. He was responsible for the conception of the Socratic dialogue, his method of teaching. He never wanted to "teach at" his students. That would be to instill doctrine. His pet hate.

Instead, he wanted to guide his students to discover their answers for themselves. He did this through a method called "Socratic questioning," which set out to uncover assumptions and unexamined beliefs and then to think about the implications of those beliefs—all this to really test whether the answers made sense.

This form of questioning became the backbone of law studies (and *Suits* scriptwriters) and was later picked up by the world of psychotherapy, including cognitive behavioral therapy, in the 1960s—which is how I became interested in the technique.

As prescribed by Socratic dialogue, I focus on the **"When?" "What?" "How?"** and **"Where?"** questions in my clinical work. I choose not to delve into the **"Why?"** question because, in my experience, it often leads down a path that goes both everywhere and nowhere:

Why are we here?

Why am I alive?

Why am I like this?

Why can't I be
like those people?

Why me?

Why? Why? Why?

ANSWER: NO REASON.
IT JUST IS. ADAPT!

The key message here is that you need to, and can, learn to adapt. On the evolution of species, Charles Darwin is often described as saying, "Only the fittest survive." What he was actually saying was, "The most adaptive survive."

Look at cockroaches. They have been around for 320 million years—they watched the dinosaurs come and go. They are still with us today, and apparently resistant to every new insect spray on the market. Now that's adaptive!

EVOLUTION IS ADAPTATION.

CHAPTER TWO

IT'S ALL CONNECTED

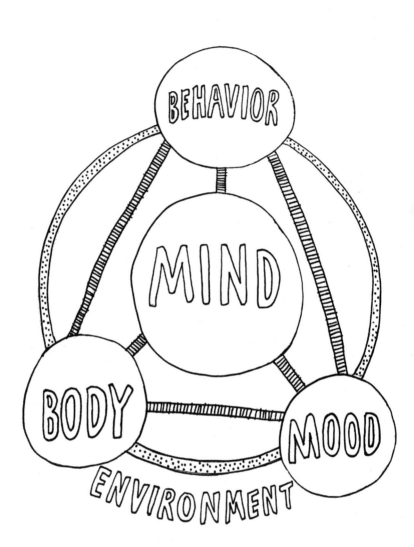

When I'm teaching I like to start off with the diagram opposite. This is a very standard template that explains the basis of cognitive behavioral therapy and how it all works. It is simple, and in its simplicity lies Aaron Beck's genius. I describe it this way—I hope Dr. Beck would approve.

The first thing to remember is that our heads are attached to our shoulders. Not only that, but the brain is in charge of everything. It's not called the "headquarters" for nothing.

All of our physical sensations (body), everything we do (behavior), everything we feel (mood), and our thinking (mind) are all inextricably linked to the brain. And all of these interact with the world around us (environment).

> We could say, "I am a brain," but
> humans prefer to say, "I _have_ a
> brain," hanging on to the belief
> that the "I" is the self, and the
> self is a separate entity. This
> separate entity is where the soul
> supposedly lives—though that
> debate would require another book.

BODY

This is our physiology, everything to do with the body. Everything we can see: legs, hands, toes, breasts, teeth, etc. Then there is everything we can't see: hormones, neurotransmitters, chromosomes, biochemicals, DNA, and so on. All of our physiology is at our fingertips, and yet there is so much we don't know about it.

The illustration opposite shows how the body responds when under alert, or the "survival response." When faced with a perceived threat, your body prepares you to go on attack (fight), run away (flight), or try to make yourself invisible (freeze).

SURVIVAL RESPONSE

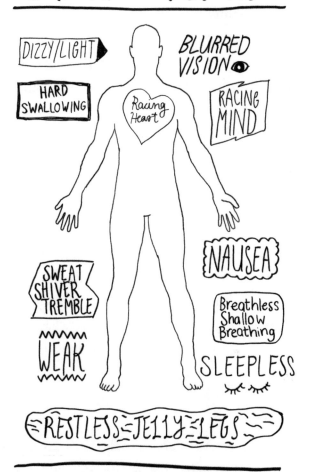

FIGHT/FLIGHT/FREEZE

Some of the physical reactions that can occur
as part of your body's "survival response"—
preparing you to fight, flee, or freeze.

This is the same response that occurs when humans describe feeling anxious.

If you become unwell, for instance with the flu, you experience all the physical symptoms associated with it: sneezing, coughing, nose running, head blocked (body). In response to this, you probably wrap yourself up and go to bed (behavior).

Then, lying in bed and not being able to get out and do the things you enjoy, you start to feel miserable (mood). Sometimes, while lying there, you also start to experience the fear of missing out (FOMO) and how none of your friends have come to visit you. Your emotions can be impacted further, making you feel even more miserable (mood).

Hopefully you are starting to see what I mean about everything being inextricably linked.

BEHAVIOR

Let's use exercise as an example. Let's say you like to go for a run or go to the gym several times a week. One day, while out running, you sprain your ankle and have to have it wrapped up (body). This means no exercise for some time. You may start to worry that you are going to get fat and out of condition (mind). These thoughts can then create discomfort and/or anxiety (mood).

When you exercise, your body releases bio-chemicals called endorphins, which have a positive effect on your feelings. Because you are not running, you are not getting those endorphins or any of the other physical benefits of exercise (body), and you worry that you are going to turn into a fat slob (mood).

MOOD

In the developed world we are becoming increasingly obsessed with mood. We have lists of all sorts of possible mood disorders—anxiety, depression, bipolar, to name but a few. Pills to take you up, to take you down, to level you out, to take the edge off. Name it, there is undoubtedly a pill for it.

This is not a new thing. Most cultures have long had drugs to help people alter their state of consciousness and, in turn, their emotions: these include opium, peyote, marijuana, alcohol, tobacco, and many more. It is a very, very long and ancient list. However . . .

Making billions out of the manufacturing of pharmaceuticals and criminalizing what comes out of Mother Nature's garden is new.

The other manifestation of our fascination with all things emotional is the arts: love poetry, melancholic poetry, music about love and loss, more loss and more love, novels, painting, comedy, dance. The wonderful world of the arts.

I love all of these aspects of life, but the scientific reality is that emotions are about neurotransmitters and hormones. They involve mood-regulation systems, dopamine, serotonin, adrenaline, and a whole lot of other bits and pieces. Too much of one, too little of another, and these extremely complex systems can go wrong.

I never cease to be amazed by the way human beings become so indignant if the brain runs out of juice and is unable to work to full capacity. This is what we call depression. When the depressed first come to see me in my clinical rooms, they often don't want to believe that they are afflicted. They might say, "I can't be depressed. I don't want to be depressed. I *shouldn't* be depressed."

When I suggest that they will probably need to take some time off work or study, they say, "I don't have time." Yet if they had been in a major car accident and their back were in traction, there would be no doubt that rest and convalescence would be required.

The brain is the most sophisticated and delicate of all the organs. In fact, it is in charge of all the other organs, and yet it is rarely granted permission to not be OK. Go figure!

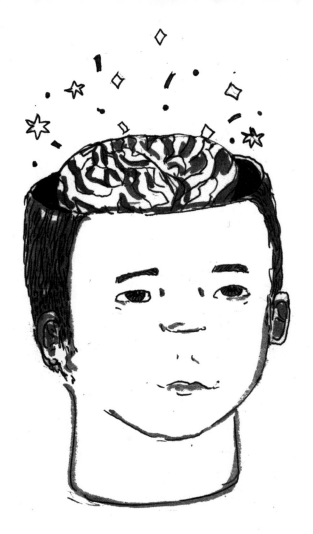

I have done a lot of work in my career on the stigma that is attached to mental health/illness. In my experience there are two forms of stigma.

First, there is the internal stigma. Thoughts such as: "I'm a failure," "I'm weak."

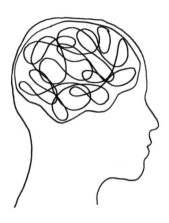

Given the profound complexity of
the brain, it stands to reason that
things can, and do, go wrong!

Second, there is external stigma and the fear of
it: "What will people think if they know I have a
mental illness?," "They will think I'm crazy," "I will
lose my job!" And so on and so forth. Again, none of
this would be an issue with a broken back!

There can be no doubt that stigma plays a
massive part in inhibiting people from getting the
help they need, from continuing to participate in
the recommended treatments, and hence from
maintaining wellness.

When your brain becomes exhausted, its
chemistry changes (body). If you work or study
for long hours at a stretch, your sleep can become
disturbed (body and behavior). Brain fatigue and

lack of refreshing sleep (body) results in flattened spirits (mood) and impacts your attention span and concentration (mind and body).

Frustrating thoughts about not being able to concentrate create more adrenaline (body), which can be distressing (mood), and around and around it goes, like a spiral of dominoes.

MIND

For the purposes of this book, the mind is the most important aspect of a human being. It incorporates beliefs, spirituality, values, attitudes, creativity, and communication. (I have distinguished spirituality and beliefs because in many cultures spirituality is considered a separate entity. In my opinion spirituality is a belief system and hence a cognitive process. You are, of course, entitled to your own opinion on this very controversial matter.)

Thought is a very intricate and infinitely complex process of the brain. It enables us to make sense of the world we experience, to interpret and negotiate. Hence it is essential for our ability to adapt. It is an integral part of our survival. Go back to that domino spiral and add another 10 squillion dominoes and I think we might be getting a little closer to this phenomenal network.

Going back to the exercise example: it's been three days now; you're still in bed, coughing and sneezing with the occasional bit of wheezing (body).

You go to the bathroom to grab some cough medicine and happen to notice the scale. You get on it (behavior), and yes, you've increased in weight (body). This, of course, can be easily accounted for by no exercise and comfort-eating chocolate ice cream and pizza (behavior and body).

OMG, I'm huge! you think to yourself. *I'm so fat and ugly, and I'm never going to stop growing! I'll be fatter than anyone I know! This is a disaster. I hate myself. I'll never be able to go out again* (mind).

Then, in a nanosecond, you feel terrible, your mood drops further, and you become anxious about this perceived never-ending weight gain (mood).

You go back to the bedroom, switch your phone off (behavior), and cry (mood and body). *My life is a mess!* (mind). This thinking spiral can go on indefinitely. More dominoes, more negative thinking, more distress. This small example illustrates the power of thought and its ability to trigger all of those behavioral, emotional, and biological responses.

Here again you get to see that
how you think influences how you
feel. So it makes sense that if you
understand how you *think*, you will
be able to manage how you *feel*.

As you can now observe, these four different domains—body, behavior, mood, and mind—make up who we are. They all impact on each other. They do NOT operate in isolation. *Because the head is attached to the body.*

CHAPTER THREE

SIMPLE AS ABC

ACTIVATING
- actual event/reality
- immediate
interpretations of event

BELIEFS
- evaluations
- rational
- irrational

CONSEQUENCES
- emotions
- behavior
- physical sensations

I t really is as simple as ABC. The ABC model was first constructed by Albert Ellis, the founder of rational emotive behavior therapy.

The illustration opposite shows the process of how we, as humans, think and respond. Body, mood, and behavior (using this model) are now classified as responses (C).

The mind (B) is primarily responsible for activating the responses, based on beliefs that may be rational (helpful and reality-based) or irrational (emotive and unhelpful). The activating event (A) is our reality. It is what the brain evaluates prior to creating a response.

CHAPTER FOUR

THE PART REALITY PLAYS

The first thing I would like to emphasize is that *"reality" is not the problem.* When people come to see me professionally, their assumption is that it is their life that is a mess, their situation that is a disaster, and thus that is the problem they are seeking help for.

This is an incorrect assumption, no matter how true it feels.

Reality just is, and shit happens!

As Shakespeare's Hamlet says: "There is nothing either good or bad, but thinking makes it so." You see, how we think about a situation determines how we will respond to it. So, it is how you think that dictates your responses.

"If I understand how I think, I get to choose how I feel."

SHIT HAPPENS.

It is the type of response that is the problem. People decide to get therapy because they feel bad (mood); they are experiencing a lot of biological symptoms—e.g., irritable bowel, fatigue, headaches, and so on (body). They might be drinking too much or eating too much or gambling too much or worrying too much (behavior). These are the experiences that bring people to the point where they seek professional help.

As long as you are alive, reality is going to throw shit your way. I was diagnosed with breast cancer a few years ago, and that was the reality. It was scary, but throwing a tantrum and feeling sorry for myself and screaming at the universe that this was unfair was going to change nothing. The fact was I had cancer. So I tried my best to go with the flow, followed the directions of my specialists, kept laughing, and eventually wrote a book. My response to the reality seems to have worked, because I am still here seven years later to tell the tale.

So, reality just *is*. It rains when you're going to the school dance; your car breaks down on the way to your graduation; the airport is closed on your way to a family reunion. There are literally millions of possibilities—all great inconveniences. You feel terrible, you feel frustrated, disappointed, furious, all of the above.

You cannot change the reality; it just is. *You* are the one who has to adapt!

What you *can* change, however, is what you are thinking about the reality. Essentially, the goal cannot be to change the reality, because the reality *just is.* You have power over how you evaluate the reality. How you think about what has happened or is happening. And then, how you respond.

If we go back to the rain-soaked dance night, you can cry, you can scream, you can hate the world. Or you can procure a stylish raincoat and an extra-large umbrella.

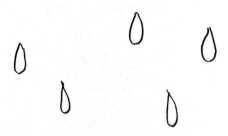

After all, it's only water.
How bad can that be?

In summary: how we think, what we think, when we think those things, how we evaluate the reality, creates how we feel and how we behave.

CHAPTER FIVE

THOUGHT CONTENT

I place an enormous amount of emphasis on the content of thought. I'm interested not just in how you're thinking but also *what* you're thinking.

When we are thinking and, in particular, thinking about ourselves, each thought is a silent conversation with the self.

If your thoughts are positive, hopeful, and optimistic—fabulous! Because as your thoughts move about and become repetitive, they form belief systems. They kindle tracks in your brain that act as pathways to how you feel about yourself, your relationships, and your place in the world.

The reverse also applies. (Flick the domino spiral in the opposite direction.) If your thoughts are negative, self-loathing, and pessimistic, this, too,

THE TALK SHOW OF THE
MIND

can become a lifetime habit for evaluating yourself.

Of course, the origins of the way you think are to do with a combination of nature and nurture, and how the two interact during your lifetime. This is called **epigenetics**.

COMPUTER-MIND ANALOGY

If you think about your brain processing information like a computer, the metaphor would be as follows:

- You have a "hard drive," where all your core beliefs and values are stored from way back when. Your early life history, your role modeling, your value system.
- Then there is the "software package," where your rules of living and your attitudes are stored. These rules often present in your thinking as the "if-thens." There you are as a child learning about how the world and the people in it work. You notice that if you behave in a certain way, then your mother gets very angry. If you behave in a different way, then your mother appears pleased. Another

important set of tools for negotiating your environment.

- Then there is the "screen." This is where all your automatic thoughts are displayed. These are the thoughts you are conscious of in your daily life.

THOUGHT INTERFERENCE

Continuing with the computer metaphor, if you have the equivalent of a "virus" in your feedback system, your thoughts become irrational. These irrational thoughts create exaggerated emotions. However, you believe them to be true. Because why wouldn't you?

Nobody wakes up in the morning and thinks to themselves, *Mmm, I should go and see a therapist, fork out a lot of money, and make sure my thoughts are true.* Because 90% of the time the brain is giving us accurate, factual information. For example, there is a chair—if I sit in the chair, I will have a place to rest. There is a door—if I open that, I will be able to go through to the next room. There is a red light—this is where I need to stop.

People don't initially come to therapy because they are checking the accuracy of their thoughts. They come because of how they are feeling, physically and/or emotionally.

As humans, the only way we know that what we experience of reality is the truth is by trusting the sensory inputs of the brain.

COGNITIVE PSYCHOLOGY

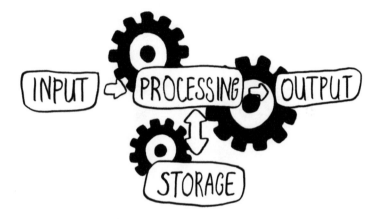

Why would you ever question any information your brain is giving you? You wouldn't. So, the **thought viruses** remain unquestioned, but they are distorting the way you think about yourself and the world and leaving you often unhappy and dissatisfied.

CHAPTER SIX

HOW TO RECOGNIZE A THOUGHT VIRUS

The school of thought that makes up cognitive behavioral therapy talks about thought viruses as "thinking errors" or **cognitive distortions**. I have nicknamed them "the viruses in your computer."

What follows is a recognized list of cognitive distortions. I will take you through each of them and explain how they affect your thinking and play havoc with your daily life.

1. NEGATIVE MENTAL FILTER

This distortion is quite self-explanatory. A **negative mental filter** means that whenever you think about your life, you look through a set of lenses that makes the world look dark and unforgiving. It is the opposite of looking at the world through "rose-colored glasses," where, no matter how bad things are, the person always sees the best and the most positive, at times to their disadvantage.

The negative way of perceiving the world is debilitating because, no matter what you are

A negative mental filter distorts
your perception of the world.

thinking about or planning to do, the negative filter clouds your thoughts with scenarios of everything that can go wrong. You consistently dwell on the negative. The thoughts then remind you of all your faults and why you will never achieve.

What a downer! What a struggle! Every day, from the moment you wake up, this thought process pours freezing water over every idea and every aspiration you have. Not just that, but when you consider starting a relationship with someone, you also get a whole lot of thoughts thundering through, reminding you that you are really not worthy, so don't even bother!

The point to remember is that these are just thoughts. They are communications to you from inside your head. They do not exist in the real world. They are a function of perception clouded by a negative filter. If you believe them, you are trapped.

However, you can choose not to believe them.

As we move through each of these distortions, I am going to provide you with suggestions on how to manage them.

Your views of yourself and the world
are reflections of your own thoughts.

**Tip #1: How to manage the
negative mental filter**

- Look at the bigger picture; consider all
  the facts.
- Are you so focused on the negatives, you
  have overlooked the positives?
- Could you find a more balanced way of
  approaching this problem?

2. ALL-OR-NOTHING THINKING

All-or-nothing thinking is also known as **black-and-white thinking**. People will often say with pride, "I'm a very black-and-white thinker. It's right, or it's wrong. I don't like messing with the middle ground."

This is all very well, but the problem with this kind of thinking is that it is so inflexible. It doesn't equip you to deviate or just roll with the punches. The universe is full of change and things that you aren't expecting, so hanging on to rigid belief systems is going against the flow of life. It leaves you unprepared to deal with anything slightly outside of your expected norm.

I think of earthquake-proofing buildings when I think of this cognitive error. Buildings and bridges these days cannot be rigid, or they will collapse under **strain** and pressure. Instead, they are built to be flexible so that they can tolerate sudden and unexpected change.

BLACK-AND-WHITE
THINKERS,
YIN AND YANG
COULD NEVER
BE TOGETHER,
AS THEY COULDN'T
MAKE ENDS MEET.

> Life is about being resilient to strain and discomfort. This is adaptation, essential for your survival!

Strain, not stress

I would like to introduce you to the importance of the word "strain." Hans Selye, the recognized founder of stress research, was at a conference once and couldn't find the word he needed for "strain." He was speaking one language, the audience spoke another, and his seminar was going through translation booths.

Eventually he arrived at the word "stress." He was later to regret choosing this word because it did not accurately describe what he was trying to communicate. The word he was looking for was "strain."

This is important. Why?

Because what has happened is that "stress" has ended up with a whole lot of subjective interpretations:

- *Positive* stress is when you do adrenaline sports and you're a hero.

- *Negative* stress is when you can't cope, feel distress, and hence are perceived as weak.

Lots of value judgments!

Subsequently, we began to use the word "stress" to mean both stress and strain. People throughout the developed world constantly talk about how stressed they are and how they can't cope.

The belief that you are unable to cope is actually created by your *perceived* inability to cope, not the reality.

Strain, on the other hand, just *is*.

It is neutral—there are no value judgments!

I use the following metaphor to explain. Imagine two very large trucks parked back-to-back. They are tied together via a piece of rope attached to each truck's tow bar. They both drive off in opposite directions, and the rope is pulled and pulled and pulled—and eventually, because of the force, the

STRAIN

rope breaks. This is strain. It's physics.

It is a fact. *It just is.* No judgments, no weakness, just fact. That is what strain is about. When you do something that you enjoy, or that you don't enjoy, or when you have an emotional reaction to something that you find difficult, these all place strain on your system. As a result of the strain, your system can shut down.

If your thought process is not flexible, you are less equipped to bounce back from strain. You need flexibility of thought in order to survive. All-or-nothing or black-and-white thinking does not allow this flexibility.

Tip #2: How to challenge all-or-nothing thinking

- Is this situation really all that bad?
- Is there a different way to look at this situation?
- Could my extreme view be more flexible?

These questions will lead you to explore ways of thinking that are not only more rational but also more helpful.

3. DISCOUNTING THE POSITIVES

This is when you insist that your accomplishments or positive qualities don't count. It is very similar to the negative mental filter. Imagine the combination of the two. The negative mental filter encourages a process of discounting everything you do. Not only do you predict that your attempts to accomplish anything are going to fail but also any achievements you have ever had are minimized.

This means that you don't look back and think, *I have done this and done that, so therefore I must be OK.*

Instead, you look back and discount anything you have ever done and only focus on what you *don't* have and what you have *not* achieved.

In today's society you are constantly exposed through all forms of media to what you could have but don't. You can look through magazines and see a Cartier watch worth more than you could earn in five years. Then you flick the page and see a Maserati car worth more than you could earn in fifteen years, then a mansion costing more than a lifetime's wages. Symbols of prestige and status. All screaming, *If you don't have me, you're a failure!*

What bullshit! If you buy in to that way of think-ing, and constantly discount what you have made of your life, where is the win? There isn't one. You are encouraged to aspire for these status symbols, but all that does is rob you of contentment and happiness. Think about this wonderful quote:

"COMPARISON IS THE THIEF OF JOY."
— THEODORE ROOSEVELT

Letting go of this set of beliefs is liberating. You get to relish what you have done. You get to believe that you are OK, which is what we all aspire to—and that is a need, not a want.

4. OVERGENERALIZING

Overgeneralizing is a **perceptual filter** that occurs when you look at one negative event in your life as being a predictive indicator of all things that will follow. For instance, you don't do too well on a particular exam. This then becomes "proof" that anything else you attempt will fail—so why bother?

Talk about a belief that stops you from believing in yourself. It stops you from seeing a new beginning. It prevents you from moving on. This belief says that if you make *one* mistake, you must be a complete, total, and absolute failure.

No realistic perspective can ever be gleaned through this filter. You have a relationship, and it doesn't work out—something that happens to people every day. When you look at your life through this filter, you are convinced that there is no point in having another relationship, because it

IF THERE WERE NO POINT,

I COULDN'T HAVE DRAWN THIS.

will inevitably turn to crap as well. So let's avoid the pain of another breakup by never having another relationship. Now there's a recipe for a happy life, I don't think!

Situations in your life, and especially your relationships with others, all have something unique about them. When you identify these unique aspects with clarity, you can learn where things went wrong and how things can be improved the next time.

Overgeneralizing shuts all those doors of opportunity—doors to new experiences. Everything looks the same, everybody is the same, and the color is 150 shades of gray. So why bother?

Another very unhelpful perceptual filter.

Tip #3: How to avoid overgeneralizing

- Focus on the specific.
- Ask yourself: What are the facts? And what are my interpretations?
- Am I applying one example to all examples?

5. MAGNIFICATION/ CATASTROPHIZING

This is one of the most common viruses that I hear about. Every day in my clinic, I see the enormous negative impact of this distorted perceptual filter and, consequently, the enormous positive impact when the filter is dissolved.

The cognitive school of thought defines **magnification** or **catastrophizing** as a scenario in which everything, no matter how tiny, feels huge, terrible, and impossible to fix.

An old English saying describes this phenomenon as "making mountains out of molehills." I believe that saying describes this filter well. The fact is there is no way some velvety little mammal, tunneling away beneath the golf course, is ever going to be able to create a mountain.

Yet, every time you catastrophize a situation, you are making a mountain out of a molehill. The even sillier thing is that you believe what you are telling yourself—and therein lies the problem.

> You believe these thought
> viruses to be true. But in the
> real and rational world, moles
> do not build mountains.

This is the other thing that we know about the thought viruses: they contaminate your rational thoughts and convince you that irrational thoughts are true.

In my clinical practice I have observed that, in the world of teenagers and young adults, catastrophizing is of epidemic proportions. One of the biggest reasons for this is the significance assigned to comments and interactions on social media.

The most damaging aspect of catastrophizing is the profound undermining of resilience. When someone believes a situation is impossible, they don't even try to overcome it.

A common scenario

One young adult meets another young adult (opposite sex, same sex, transgender, nonbinary, gender fluid . . . whatever), an attraction occurs, cell phone numbers are exchanged, and a text relationship begins.

Next day:

A young person (One) makes telephone contact with their best friend (Bestie).

> **One:** You won't believe it! I met this fantastic guy. He's amazing. We spoke for ages, and—wait for it—he asked me for my number.
> **Bestie:** Wow, he asked you! That's amazing! He must be really into you.
> **One:** I know. He asked me out of nowhere. I didn't even have to ask him. I'm so excited.
> **Bestie:** Did he text you?
> **One:** He has, isn't that amazing? He said, "nice to meet u" with two big XXs and three little xxxs.
> **Bestie:** You mean XXxxx! That's incredible!

Second day:

One calls Bestie, sobbing.

Bestie: OMG, what's wrong?

One: I texted him back and signed off with two big XXs and two small xxs because I didn't want to look needy. I sent it at about nine this morning. I waited all day, but he didn't text me back until six tonight.

Bestie: What did he say?

One: He texted, "Nice to hear from u," but then signed off with two small xxs.

Bestie: Only two small xxs! Didn't you have three small ones and two big XXs yesterday? OMG!

One: (wailing, gasping for breath, on the verge of a panic attack) I know, I know. I thought he was perfect for me. I don't know why I even bother. I so desperately want him back. The chemistry was so right. We could have made a life together. I even thought about what our children would be like! I can't take this. My life may as well be over. What's the point?

Bestie: (lost for words)

Rational interpretation of the facts:

- Guy and One exchange numbers.
- Guy texts the following day. Throws in a few Xs to sign off. Two big ones and three small ones.
- One calls Bestie and relays the news.
- Bestie is pleased, as besties are.
- Following day Guy replies to text. Throws in another few xs on the sign-off.
- One calls Bestie, distraught, sobbing, and hyperventilating.

The irrational thought process convinces One that their life has no meaning: all is lost! This is where magnification plays a part. The situation is now huge and insurmountable. The worst thing that could ever be experienced.

Here we see the **magnification thought virus**, fueled by **overgeneralization** with a **negative mental filter** and **all-or-nothing thinking**, all in interaction with each other. Creating disaster, emotional pain, and hopelessness.

See how they all work together to create a perception of reality that is untrue and unhelpful.

THE PROPORTIONAL Xs

· CASUAL ·

·SUGGESTIVE?·

ahh - INTERESTED!

...DEAD IN THE WATER

Because in reality:

One meets a random guy and swaps numbers. Text interaction occurs, and it gets flirty. The next day, the guy remembers he's not so single, hides the texts from his partner, and tries to bring the conversation back into friend territory. End of story.

See the danger of overvaluing and magnification, and how it creates a false perception of reality? Worst of all, convincing you that it is true?

Tip #4: How to put things into perspective

Ask yourself:

- What is the worst possible thing that can happen?
- What is the best possible outcome?
- What is the most likely thing to happen?
- Will I care about this in five years' time?
- Is there a solution to this problem?

6. MINIMIZATION

This is sort of the opposite of magnification. **Minimization** refers to the cognitive process where you put down your achievements. You do something good, and when someone compliments you, you say, "Oh, it was nothing" or "I was just lucky." This underestimation is common with anxious and depressive thinking.

Minimization means that you
don't get to appreciate and
embrace any of your achievements
because you're too busy pointing
out that you're a fraud.

---

7. JUMPING TO CONCLUSIONS (ASSUMPTIONS)

This thinking error creates many problems. It is such a huge contaminant of rational thought, it seduces you into believing it is true. It comes in two forms: **mind reading** and **fortune telling**.

Minimization is a thought virus in which you
make your achievements small and insignificant.

Mind reading

This is when we observe the behavior of other people and then interpret what they are thinking.

These interpretations convince you that other people are thinking negatively about you, and then the discomfort begins. This creates feelings of insecurity, which then convinces you even more that they are thinking negatively about you.

The other thing that occurs when you believe you know what someone is thinking is that you start believing they are thinking the same negative thoughts that you have about yourself. Now, that is so spooky it verges on the ridiculous.

Imagine this. You are in a room full of people, and they are all thinking about you. And not just that. In fact, they are thinking about you *exactly* the same way you think about yourself.

How likely is that? Statistically, it is not even remotely probable! It is just not happening!

This belief that you know what people are thinking about you can create all sorts of internal distress. The reality is that you have no idea what anyone else is thinking, and chances are they are thinking about their own worries or concerns and nothing whatsoever about you. I pose the question, "Can you read people's minds?"

I am confident the answer is "No."

Nobody can read minds. All the research in the world—twin studies, clairvoyance studies—suggests that it is impossible for people to read others' minds.

You are not a mind reader, but this thought virus convinces you that you are. Once again proving how powerful irrational thoughts can be. Because these thoughts create feelings, and when they do, you become convinced that the thoughts must be true.

Beliefs are not facts, and the feelings that result from those beliefs are not facts, either!

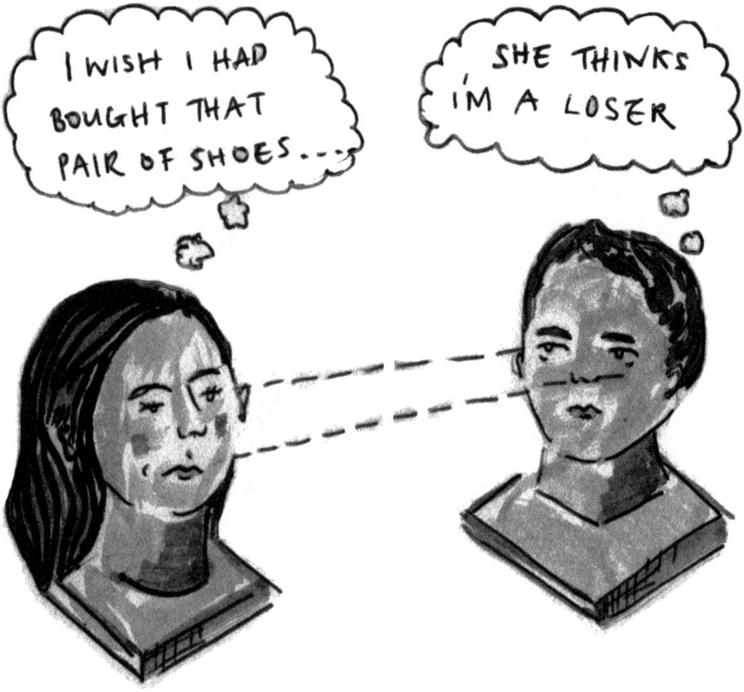
I WISH I HAD BOUGHT THAT PAIR OF SHOES...
SHE THINKS I'M A LOSER

Fortune telling

By "fortune telling" I mean that very special gift when you believe you can see into the future. For example: "There's no way I'll ever get a girlfriend. I'll be on my own forever."

I often jokingly say to my clients, "Well, if you are so good at fortune telling, how about you predict the winning lottery numbers?" Of course, this is not possible.

Fortune telling is not real or based in fact. It is yet another example of an irrational belief system.

In the context of "fortune telling," the negative mental filter guarantees traveling down a thought spiral of disastrous outcomes. Then "magnification" steps in, which guarantees that the disastrous outcome will indeed be big and that you won't cope with it.

Negative fortune telling is something that worriers do all the time. Life becomes constantly difficult to navigate because everything is perceived as and predicted to be difficult. That does not mean life *is* difficult; it is just that negative filter influencing your thought patterns yet again.

You can choose between believing what is based on irrational thinking and believing only what is true and factual. Which makes more sense?

Tip #6: Remember, you cannot predict the future

- Ask yourself: Can you really read into the future?
- Just because you feel something is about to happen, that does not make it so.
- How does it help you to imagine bad things are about to happen?

"That won't work out, so there's no point in trying".
"I'd make a mess of that. I'm not ready yet."
"I'll always be alone"
"Nothing will ever work out for me"
"I'm not dating that person. It would never work out."
"I'll go, but I won't enjoy myself"

8. EMOTIONAL REASONING

In the early days of my career, I never quite knew what the thinking error **emotional reasoning** was about. It wasn't obvious to me like the mind reading and fortune telling thinking errors. My clients, too, seemed to find it easier to understand how mind reading and fortune telling were unhelpful and not based in fact.

With a little bit of practice they could guide their thinking away from those particular false beliefs.

So what do we mean by "emotional reasoning"? And how does it play a part in our harmful thought processes?

Emotional reasoning = evaluating situations by how we feel.

Still I didn't get it. Don't we all evaluate situations by how we feel?

For example: *"I met my gf's parents. I could feel immediately that they hated me."* Seems reasonable. You feel a vibe, check out the body language, do a bit of mind reading, and you have it figured out. *Copy that.*

On first consideration it's hard to comprehend how emotional reasoning impacts negatively on balanced, rational thinking. However, it does, and in my clinical experience, the impact is probably greater than from other thought viruses.

Back to One and the texts

One magnifies the situation with the random text. She blows it out of proportion—magnifies it—and becomes miserable about her life and future. She feels this way because of how she is thinking. Once people feel and believe that they are unlovable, they convince themselves that all their predictions will come true.

The feelings are then perceived as evidence of the truth. Again, not true. Feelings are only reflections of thought.

FEELINGS ARE NOT FACTS.

Here is a quotation from David Burns, from his book *Feeling Good: The New Mood Therapy*. I turn to this paragraph a lot when I am working with people in similar situations, as it describes exactly what I am trying to convey:

> *Even though your depressing thoughts may be distorted they nevertheless create a powerful illusion of truth. Let me expose the basis for the deception in blunt terms—your feelings are not facts! In fact, your feelings, per se, don't even count—except as a mirror of the way you are thinking. If your perceptions make no sense, the feelings they create will be as absurd as the images reflected in the trick mirrors at an amusement park.*

> *But these abnormal emotions feel just as valid and realistic as the genuine feelings created by undistorted thoughts, so you automatically attribute truth to them. This is why depression is such a powerful form of mental black magic.*

Tip #7: Remember,
feelings are not facts

- Perception and reality are linked, but they are not the same.
- Just because you feel bad, this does not mean your perceptions are correct.
- Separate your feelings from the facts, to prevent confusion.

9. COGNITIVE REASONING

This is a challenging thought virus because it challenges the difference between what you believe and what is true. (Beliefs are not facts.) Now that's thought-provoking.

If I were to say to you, "I believe the world is round," my statement would be redundant. It is a fact that the world is round, so what I believe is irrelevant.

We used to believe the world was
flat. It isn't! Beliefs are not facts.

Another thing humans used to believe was that Earth was at the center of the universe, and that the Sun, Moon, stars, and planets all revolved around us. Nowadays we know that this isn't true, and the fact is that Earth revolves around the Sun. But back in the 1600s the famous scientist Galileo was imprisoned by the Roman Catholic Church for promoting and teaching what later became accepted as fact. He remained under house arrest for nearly a decade, until his death in 1642—all because the leaders of the day believed something that wasn't true.

Religion is another example of the power of beliefs. Christians, Jews, and Muslims all believe in a higher power, but no one can prove that their God is the "right" one and that everyone else has got it wrong. Religious beliefs are based on faith rather than evidence.

What we are exploring in *The Book of Knowing* are not philosophical beliefs but your beliefs about yourself and whether they work for or against your sense of well-being. If you believe and feel that you are not good enough, then you will consequently feel bad and worthless. The feelings reinforce your beliefs, and the beliefs reinforce your feelings. You will then behave in a way that fits your beliefs that you are unacceptable.

Here is an example of the negative consequences of cognitive reasoning. *How can I make friends and be a member of a group when I believe I am not acceptable? It's best not to even try, because I predict that I will be rejected, and that will be too painful. Best to avoid the pain. Best to stay isolated and alone.*

So your cognitive reasoning and your emotional reasoning join up with all the other thought viruses, and before you know it, you have nowhere to turn. Cognitively trapped—a prisoner of your own self-beliefs. Imprisoned by them, creating walls that don't exist in the real world.

Why do you remain a prisoner
of your beliefs when the
door is wide open?

10. PERSONALIZATION

In the field of psychology, the cognitive definition of **personalization** is simple.

Personalization = blaming ourselves unfairly for something for which we are not totally responsible.

Examples include:

My boyfriend has left me, and it's all my fault.

I didn't get into the school show—it's because I am a terrible actor.

My favorite example utilizes The Slamming Door. Imagine yourself sitting at a desk: you might be at work, or studying, or at home. A significant person (your teacher or your boss) walks past you to go into their office or into another room, doesn't say hello, and then the door slams. You personalize the situation, and **negative automatic thinking** kicks in.

Negative automatic thinking looks like this:

OMG!!! What have I done?

It must have been something really bad, because I didn't even get a hello.

I could see by the look in her eye that something is wrong. She is probably thinking she can't stand me.

I must be so useless. I'll probably be kicked out, and then what will I do? I'll never get another chance like this one.

This is a disaster! What will my family think? They'll think I can never stick with anything, that I am useless, and they will give up on me.

What if I can't find anywhere else? This was my only chance. I'm doomed! I will never succeed.

Now let's play a round of spot the thinking errors:

OMG!!! What have I done? (personalizing/magnification/emotional reasoning)

It must have been something really bad, because I didn't even get a hello. (personalizing/negative mental filter)

I could see by the look in her eye that something is wrong. She is probably thinking she can't stand me. (mind reading/negative mental filter/personalizing/ fortune telling)

I must be so useless. I'll probably be kicked out, and then what will I do? I'll never get another chance like this one. (fortune telling/negative mental filter/all-or-nothing thinking)

This is a disaster! What will my family think? They'll think I can never stick with anything, that I am useless, and they will give up on me. (magnification/mind reading/fortune telling/negative labeling/negative mental filter)

What if I can't find anywhere else? This was my only chance. I'm doomed! I will never succeed. (all-or-nothing thinking/fortune telling/negative mental filter/negative labeling)

Wow! Not too difficult to see the irrationality of interpreting a slamming door to mean all those things. It only takes the blink of an eye for all of these thoughts to turn up like a tsunami, bringing devastation in its wake. Remember: none of these thoughts exist in fact. They are based on misperception and emotional reasoning. Rational thought is washed out by the sheer force of the negative beliefs.

This example and the outcome (see opposite) is taken from my practice, from a client experiencing stress in her workplace.

The facts of The Slamming Door

1. Boss got to work late, having been stuck in traffic, and was running late for an international call.

2. Breeze from an open window caught the door and blew it shut.

3. Boss finished call and eventually said, "Good morning."

4. The End.

Tip #8: It's not all about you.
Things to consider:
- What exactly might I have done wrong?
- Are there other possible explanations?

11. "SHOULD" STATEMENTS— ACCOMPANIED BY THE "SHOULD," "MUST," AND "HAVE TO" SISTERS

Let me explain. As words, "should," "must," and "have to" all aid us in creating unhealthy emotional, biological, and behavioral responses.

A young client, battling with the demands of "should" statements, described them this way: "When I hear those thoughts coming through, I label them as the "should," "must," and "have to" sisters. That way," she said, "I don't take the thoughts seriously and can laugh them off."

The table below shows how destructive the "should," "must," and "have to" statements can be. Particularly with regard to how you feel about yourself, other people, and the world.

Thoughts	Effects
I should have	guilt/regret
I shouldn't have	guilt/self-loathing
They should have	anger/frustration/disappointment
They shouldn't have	resentment/anger/frustration
I have to	pressure/tension/obligation
I must	more pressure/more tension

Now there's a bucket of fun! All of those negative emotions—so much tension and distress. Amazing that we still attribute value to those words.

When I started teaching about the detrimental impact of the word "should," I was working with a dentist who was very ordered, very controlled, and a negative perfectionist. He was horrified when I suggested that he eliminate the words "should," "must," and "have to" from his thinking vocabulary. He was fearful that he would become demotivated and hence fail.

Lots of people fear this loss of motivation. However, fear-driven motivation makes people ill. True motivation comes from the desire to *do* something. The dentist also believed that without the word "should," the world would be in anarchy.

Which brings us to the two classifications used in **cognitive theory** when discussing the word "should."

Instructional "shoulds"

These are what are used to teach children. For example, children "should" be taught never to put a fork into an electrical outlet. Teaching that hopefully minimizes the risk of the child getting electrocuted. So it is a helpful "should."

Instructional "shoulds" are also used when providing instructions, say for the use of a computer or some piece of machinery. For example, "You should always back up your hard drive before updating your computer system software." Again, this is helpful, fact-based information.

Instructional "shoulds" are helpful.

INSTRUCTIONAL "SHOULD" IS A MUSIC TEACHER WHO SWEETENS THE TUNE OF THE "SHOULD SISTERS," SOFTENING THEIR NOTES FROM "SHOULDS" TO MELODIC & SOOTHING "COULDS."

Moralistic "shoulds"

Here is where the problems occur. For example, "You should do it my way because my way is the right way." "You shouldn't believe in that god because my god is the right one." "You shouldn't be wearing that brand of jeans because they aren't cool."

Moralistic "shoulds" are based on values, beliefs, and expectations.
Question: Whose beliefs are the right ones?
Answer: None of them.
Beliefs are not facts.

So what can you do about the "should," "must," and "have to" sisters? I recommend a couple of things:

1. Be aware of the "shoulds" in your thinking. When you recognize those thoughts coming through, replace the words with something less demanding. Getting rid of the "should" from your thinking language is very liberating.

2. When you're looking for alternative words, think of words based on choice. Instead of "I *should* go on a diet," which is demanding and guilt-provoking because you didn't stick to the last one, think, "I *could* go on that diet today. I'll see how the day goes."

Can you recognize the difference between thinking words based on choice and thinking words based on demand? When you say them aloud, can you physically feel the difference? Choice words are so much better. Notice how you feel more relaxed?

I don't use the word "should" these days. It causes far too many negative emotions that I don't want or need.

12. "I CAN'T STAND IT"

Another term from the Albert Ellis school of thought, the "I can't stand it" thought virus does a lot to convince you of your inability to deal with difficult situations. Given that everyday life is full of little annoyances, it's important we learn to be resilient and tolerant in the face of them.

Tolerance is essential to your ability
to adapt to your environment
and live happily in the world.

David Burns defines it this way: "Some people get intolerant when they have to do things they don't enjoy. They tell themselves that they 'can't stand' certain things instead of acknowledging that they don't enjoy them. As a result they become frustrated and angry."

I find this thought virus very common in the teens and young adults who I work with. You guys have grown up in a technological age where everything is immediate—at the push of a button you have access to any information you want. You can go shopping without leaving your bedroom, and you can have it brought to your door with no effort. Essentially, it is possible to avoid interacting with the world if you prefer it that way—everything can be delivered to you.

Depending on the type of parents you have, if you don't want to catch a bus, they will probably be happy to drive you. If you are really fortunate, they might even buy you a car.

Perhaps you try to avoid being out in public, or you can't stand waiting. Maybe you tell yourself that having to use public transportation is the worst thing imaginable. What happens if you are seen by people you want to impress? *OMG, what will they think?*

Then this sort of thinking can kick in:

I shouldn't have to be dealing with this.

I should have my own car. I can't stand this!

This is the worst thing that could happen.

I hate this—I never want to have to do this again.

Resulting in these feelings: frustration, intolerance, anger, resentment, tension.

These thought viruses are in action: magnification, "should" statements, negative mental filter, all-or-nothing thinking.

With these thoughts you are convincing yourself that you can't possibly tolerate this situation. That you can't handle it. This leaves you with an accompanying feeling of helplessness.

I once worked with a young woman who was struggling with panic and anxiety. Nearly every time something went wrong, she would start thinking, *I can't stand this; I can't get out of this; this is a nightmare,* and would wind herself into a state of panic.

After a series of sessions spent working on "I can't stand it" and identifying the nonfactual basis of this way of thinking, she said that by challenging the inaccurate beliefs, she felt a lot more resilient and able to tolerate stressful situations. Each challenging situation she made it through gave her extra confidence. Excellent, I thought. This cognitive stuff really works!

REALITY IS RANDOM AND CHANCE.

Tip #9: Feeling frustrated is just a normal part of life

- You may not enjoy frustration, but you can stand it!
- Frustrating situations are annoying obstacles, but life is full of obstacles. The trick is how you deal with them.

If you don't accept reality for what it is, you're fucked. Because the universe doesn't care. It is not just, nor is it fair. Otherwise, bad things would not happen to good people.

CHAPTER SEVEN

WHAT NOW? HOW DOES ALL THIS THEORY WORK FOR ME?

Now that you are loaded up with knowledge (albeit something of a *Lonely Planet Guide* to the world of cognitive theory), chances are you're not entirely sure what to do with it. A bit like being all dressed up with nowhere to go!

Time to put the pieces of the puzzle into place and come out with a practical guide to rational-based thinking.

1. BODY/MIND/BEHAVIOR/MOOD

This diagram is designed to clearly illustrate how human beings engage with the world. The most important thing is that you understand that all of these elements of the equation work together. None of them operate in isolation. Feelings do not just turn up—they are generated by thought. This process is the same for all of us.

SITUATION
something <u>happens</u>

⇩

THOUGHT
the situation is <u>interpreted</u>

⇩

EMOTION
a <u>feeling</u> occurs as a
result of the thought

⇩

BEHAVIOR
an <u>action</u> takes place in
response to the emotion

REALITY → BIOLOGY
(physical sensation)

2. REALITY

With regard to reality, you may be tempted to think:

Is reality the cause of all my problems?

If my reality were better, I wouldn't feel this way!

When in fact, reality and perception are two different things.

REALITY AND PERCEPTION ARE TWO DIFFERENT THINGS.

Yes, we do all live in the same real world, and yes, it is unpredictable, and often things don't go as planned. However, despite living in the same reality as our friends and family, our individual experiences of living in the world are dictated to us by our perceptions. We negotiate the world through our perceptual reality.

Our perceptual filters are the result of our nature and nurture (epigenetics)—the values we are taught and the beliefs we acquire to negotiate our environment.

Also, our responses are a part of our evolutional design. What I mean by this is that we have a very ancient part of our brain, often referred to as the reptilian brain. This is the **amygdala**—where the survival response (fight/flight/freeze) lives. This is where your "huge" responses come from.

The frontal lobe (the key "control center" of our brain) sends a message to the amygdala. Having perceived an event as "dangerous," the amygdala fires into action, activating the fight/flight/freeze response. The amygdala does not rationalize—it is not capable of thinking or reasoning (that is the job of the frontal lobe)—it just reacts. Contemporary human beings label this "anxiety," and then "panic."

We therapists are big on the use of metaphor for teaching, and I like this one. I devised it for explaining this complex brain function. Metaphors are great for the productive use of your imagination.

Scenario one: the party

So, imagine that your amygdala is a fire station situated in the back of the brain, full of sexy fire-fighters (first response team). They sit there playing the odd game of poker, but always on the job, waiting for the alarm to go off. When the frontal lobe sends down a message, such as "threat" or "danger," the crew is prepared to leap into action, racing down that pole and into the truck, ready to extinguish the life-threatening fire.

Meanwhile, you and your frontal lobe are busy going through your wardrobe trying to decide what to wear to a party that the supposed cool kids will be attending. You rummage and rummage through all your clothes and finally decide that jeans and a shirt are the most appropriate attire.

You go to where you keep your jeans, see what's available, and think, *OMG, this is a nightmare! I only*

have Wrangler or Diesel, and everyone at the party will be wearing True Religion. This is a disaster!

I can't possibly go. I will be the most uncool person, and everyone will look at my jeans and think, "So yesterday!"

That's it. I'm not going. I don't ever want to go anywhere again. My life is ruined!

The firemen hear *"My life is ruined"* and figure that you are under threat. Down the pole they go, into the truck. Panic stations! Where is the life-threatening experience? Where are we going? Is she OK? Is her room on fire?

Message to the firefighters: "No, there isn't a fire. She is just trying to pick out the jeans everyone cool will be wearing to tonight's party."

Clearly this is not life-threatening, but the amygdala, with no capacity to reason, responded as though it were.

Back in the bedroom you behaved as though it were, because it *felt* as though it were a disaster (emotional reasoning). Not having True Religion jeans can apparently be quite a big deal these days!

> The survival mechanism is continually switched on for reasons other than life-threatening experiences. You just tell yourself that you are in danger because of your beliefs. When, really, who gives a shit what jeans you wear?

Scenario two: the movies

This is a simple example but a good one—it happens often and is worth considering.

You and your friend decide to go to the movies together. You end up falling asleep, bored and struggling to maintain any interest whatsoever. But when the lights come on, your friend is in tears and says: "That was the most powerful movie I have ever seen. It was beautiful."

How can that happen? You both heard the same music, looked at the same footage, the same actors, the same story line. The answer is: your individual perceptions of the movie and the "meaning" that you give to them define the experience for you.

Perceptual lenses

Clearly the movie meant something different to your friend than it did to you. It may have resonated with something from his childhood—there could be a multitude of reasons why he reacted differently than you. Your individual perceptions of the same reality were different.

It is helpful to liken perception to the filters in a pair of glasses. These "perceptual lenses" are made up of the following three dimensions:

1. **Meaning-giving:** This lens is made up of everything that is you—your experience of other people and of the world. That is how you attribute the meaning that generates your responses.

2. **Inference:** This lens is all about reaching a conclusion, making a well-informed guess from having read between the lines. In cognitive theory, what is explored is the inference about self: "If this is true, what does it say about me? What does it mean about me?" Because again your life experience colors this lens and often distorts the meaning given to the reality.

3. Thinking distortions (thought viruses): By now you have read the list of thinking distortions in Chapter Six. It is essential that you become familiar with that list so you can recognize them when you think them, because these are the culprits that cause the most emotional difficulty for you when you are interpreting reality. They create another set of distortions in your perceptual lenses, guaranteeing that your thoughts remain irrational and you continue believing that the irrational thinking is reality.

I would like to highlight the importance of all this new knowledge and the language we have been using.

What we are NOT talking about is the use of "positive affirmations." You know, those little sayings where you look in the mirror and repeat: "I am a child of the universe. I am special and I can love myself just for who I am." Mmm. I have an idiosyncratic explanation for this. I refer to it as "putting sugar on shit." If you were able to think in such a manner, you wouldn't be reading this book.

The cognitive method is not about gluing positive thoughts to your existing negative thought content and hoping that, fingers crossed, it will fix you. The outcome of using the cognitive approach is that your thinking does become more positive, but the most important outcome is that the thinking is more helpful, constructive, and reality-based.

CHAPTER EIGHT

SKILLS FROM THE COGNITIVE TOOL KIT

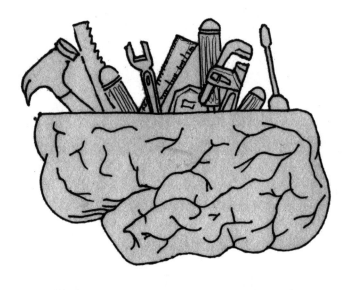

COGNITIVE

· TOOL KIT ·

The first tool in the kit is the **thought record**. This is based on the ABC model, although it includes "thought viruses." It is a bit like a thought diary, but not quite. It is how you start to apply what you have learned. Take a sheet of paper and divide it into four columns: A, B, C, and D.

COLUMN A: ACTIVATING (SITUATION/EVENT)

Column A is where you record events that bothered you throughout your day. Each event must be described factually, without feelings. It can be tricky to do initially, because it takes awhile to learn how to separate thoughts and feelings. Don't be concerned if you get the two mixed up initially.

Let's go back to the movies. Your friend noticed that you were asleep most of the time—he feels offended and upset. He goes home and writes up a thought record to help him process his feelings.

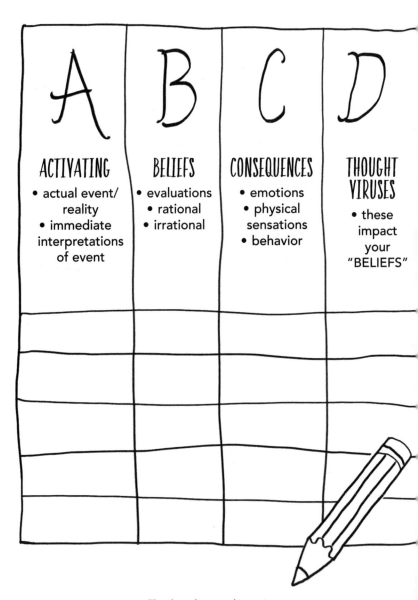

The thought record in action.

How not to describe the event

Went to the movies with my best friend today. She fell asleep and didn't watch any of the film, which really annoyed me. I found it rude and insensitive, and she didn't care about how I was feeling.

This description is full of feelings and thinking errors (mind reading/negative mental filter/personalization/emotional reasoning).

The event must be described only with factual information. The event is what actually occurred, not how you feel about the event.

How to describe the event

Went to the movies with my best friend. She fell asleep.

See the difference? Facts only!

COLUMN B: BELIEFS (AUTOMATIC THOUGHTS)

You could go to column B next, but I find most people prefer to go to column C and list their feelings first. I believe people find this easier because feelings occur so quickly after the event, and because they are often the most overwhelming part of the process.

Also, people often believe that feelings occur before beliefs.

More often than not, when I ask people what they were thinking when a particular event occurred that made them angry, they reply, "I wasn't thinking anything—I was so pissed off!" It may feel that way, but that is not scientifically correct.

Column B is where you record all of your spontaneous and automatic thoughts. It is important that you do not censor these so you get an accurate measure of how you think, not how you *think* you should think.

Do not be tempted to look at your list of thoughts and cross them out because they look "crazy." The benefit of writing them down is that you begin to expose yourself to the irrational nature of the thinking so that you can make positive changes.

So, just get all the thoughts down—as many as you can. Remember, it doesn't matter how ridiculous or irrational they look. It is the irrational thoughts that need to be worked with, so don't pretend they are not there.

The most important thing is that the experience is documented. When you become more practiced at this, you will be able to do it in your head, but initially it's best to write it down on paper (or type it into your phone if you prefer).

COLUMN C: CONSEQUENCES

Feelings/Emotions (0–100%)

annoyed

frustrated

unloved

upset

offended

angry

jealous

embarrassed

anxious

The idea here is to rate your feelings on a scale of 0-100%. What you are rating here are the **subjective units of distress** (SUDs).

What this means is if you feel an emotion particularly strongly, you would put, say, 90% next to it. That would be the measure of how much you felt that particular emotion. They are called *subjective* units of distress because they rate how you personally felt in response to the situation. They are not objective measurements that can be taken by a scientific instrument. Don't worry about how you believe you should have felt or how you think other people might have felt.

You might say, "It is ridiculous that I would feel this way about something so trivial, when there are millions of people dying of hunger in Uganda." You may even feel guilty or silly, but denying or dismissing how a situation truly made you feel won't help you evaluate the impact of your feelings and understand the thinking that creates those feelings. You have to stick with how it felt for you.

Column C (Consequences) should also include your physical sensations and your behavioral responses (what you felt in your body and how you reacted at the time).

Physical sensations (body)

This is the range of physical sensations you have when the fight/flight/freeze mechanism gets switched on. You might experience some of the following:

- racing heart
- jelly-like legs
- sweating or shivering
- dizziness/light-headedness
- mind racing
- feeling of breathlessness
- nausea/lack of appetite
- difficulty swallowing
- blurry vision

It is important to include these things on your list if they occurred, as they provide you with an understanding of how your body responds in certain situations. These physical symptoms can also act as a flag for when you are starting to become anxious or distressed.

Behavior

This is where you record what you did in response to the situation—for example, slammed the door, switched off the phone, stopped talking, threw something, started worrying. (Worry goes into the behavior column because it is considered a behavior, even though it is a thinking process.)

COLUMN D: THOUGHT VIRUSES

Back to the movies example. One of the thoughts— *She didn't care about me*—contains these thought viruses: mind reading, negative mental filter, personalization, and emotional reasoning.

After doing your thought record on this particular situation, you will have in front of you all the mechanics of your thinking and responding, right from the trigger event that activated the irrational thoughts.

You will also have all the information required to begin challenging your thinking and shifting your levels of distress, as well as a visual indication of how all these different components interact.

A COMPLETED THOUGHT RECORD

Below is an example based on a true story.

Event (A)

Lunch scheduled to meet boyfriend's mother for the first time.

Automatic negative thoughts (B)

There's no way I'm going to be able to deal with this.

I never come across well in these situations.

I will forget what I am going to say, and then I will start stuttering.

I will go red, and she'll notice that I'm shining like an overripe tomato.

She'll think: "Why is my son going out with this shining-red moron who can't even put a sentence together? He should find someone better."

I will say all the wrong things. She will be embarrassed and try to finish the lunch early.

She will make it really obvious that she wants me to leave and never wants to lay eyes on me again.

It will be the worst day of my life!

I can't stand it!

Responses (C)

Emotions/Mood (units of distress 0–100%)

anxious 90%

fearful 60%

shy 50%

embarrassed 80%

Physical sensations (body)

stomachache

heart racing

headache

shallow breathing

blushing

Behavior

worrying

making excuses

avoiding conversation

avoiding eye contact

Thought viruses at work (D)

There's no way I'm going to be able to deal with this. (fortune telling/mind reading/negative filter/over-generalizing)

I never come across well in these situations. (fortune telling/all-or-nothing thinking/negative filter)

I will forget what I am going to say, and then I will start stuttering. (fortune telling/negative filter)

I will go red, and she'll notice that I'm shining like an overripe tomato. (fortune telling/mind reading/personalizing/negative filter)

She'll think: "Why is my son going out with this shining-red moron who can't even put a sentence together? He should find someone better." (mind reading/fortune telling/negative labeling/negative filter/"should" statements/emotional reasoning)

I will say all the wrong things. She will be embarrassed and try to finish the lunch early. (fortune telling/ negative filter/mind reading/cognitive reasoning)

She will make it really obvious that she wants me to leave and never wants to lay eyes on me again. (fortune telling/mind reading/all-or-nothing thinking/ emotional reasoning/negative filter)

It will be the worst day of my life! I can't stand it! (catastrophizing/fortune telling/negative filter)

Wow, that's exhausting. I can't imagine that I would ever want to go to lunch with anyone—ever—if I felt like that.

Remember also that she hasn't even met the mother at this point. So all of this thinking creates anticipatory anxiety.

This is what worry is all about. What if this happens? And then what if that happens? Then this will happen, and then it will be a huge disaster. It is anxiety in anticipation of an event. Hence the desire to make excuses and avoid situations, and the feeling of living in dread, with sleepless nights, over something that has not yet occurred—apart from in your imagination.

Worry = the prediction of negative catastrophic outcomes.

So you can see how powerful negative/irrational thinking can be, in so many different ways, throughout all aspects of your life and your relationships.

MORE TOOLS FROM THE TOOL KIT

On the following page is a matrix that I designed to help challenge the assumed meaning of irrational thought. It provides all the main reference points that you will need to begin to challenge your negative automatic thoughts, primarily by looking at the thinking errors and understanding how irrational

A MATRIX FOR CHALLENGING IRRATIONAL THOUGHTS

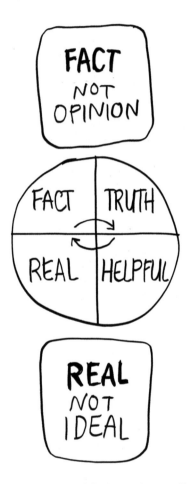

To achieve rational thinking, ask yourself:
Is my thinking based in fact, truth,
and reality? Is my thinking helpful?

they are. In other words, checking whether or not they are based in fact.

Reattributing meaning

This basically means considering possible alternative causes for events. It is also called **cognitive restructuring**, and it's an important part of what you are learning. It is a process of learning to identify and then dispute irrational thoughts (thought viruses).

The reattribution of meaning also allows you to disprove the thinking that is unhelpful for you. That is why it is important for you to be familiar with the thought viruses, so that you can learn to identify them when they occur.

How to apply the matrix

- **Fortune telling:** Is it TRUE you can predict the future? No.
- **Mind reading:** Is it a FACT that you can read people's minds? No.
- **Negative mental filter:** In the REAL world does everything you do turn out badly? No.
- **Catastrophizing:** If you blush, is that the worst

thing in the REAL world that could ever happen to you? No.

- **Cognitive reasoning:** Is it TRUE that because you believe something it is a fact? No. (Beliefs are not facts.)
- **Emotional reasoning:** If you feel something as a result of a prediction, does that make it TRUE? No. (Feelings are not facts.)
- **All-or-nothing thinking:** If you blush, does this mean that it is a FACT someone will never want to see you again? No.
- **"I can't stand it":** In the REAL world have you ever dealt with anything more difficult than meeting someone who might not like you? Of course you have, so therefore it is not true that you won't be able to stand this situation. Is thinking this way about something that has not even happened yet a HELPFUL thing to do? Definitely not!

Rational thinking challenges the irrational. The most helpful place for your thinking to be is firmly positioned in the rational.

In the RATIONAL =
TRUTH & FACT
REAL & HELPFUL

Not in the irrational, where thoughts and beliefs are based on opinions and ideals.

Let's go back to the thought record of that lunch. If it were true that the bf's mother said to her son, "Don't ever bring that girl here again. She is an idiot. You should be looking for someone in your league," that would be her *opinion*, not a *fact*.

If she did think that her son should be going out with a member of a royal family, that would be her *ideal*, not what is *real*.

Magically, with the understanding you now have, you can turn the negative automatic thoughts into rational alternative thoughts . . .

Rational alternatives

There's no way I am going to deal with this. I never come across well in these situations.

Alternative: I hope it goes OK. I feel awkward sometimes when I meet new people. (positive expectations/true)

I will forget what I am going to say, and then I will start stuttering.

Alternative: At times I get a bit forgetful, so I'll practice my breathing if I start to feel that way. (true/helpful)

I will go red, and she will notice that I'm shining like an overripe tomato.

Alternative: Sometimes I blush, but, really, how bad is that? (true/helpful)

She will think: "Why is my son going out with this shining-red moron who can't even put a sentence together? He should find someone better."

Alternative: We may not get along, but, on the other hand, we might get along well. (realistic)

I will say all the wrong things. She will be embarrassed and try to finish the lunch early.
Alternative: I'll do my best to engage in conversation. (positive intentions)

She will make it really obvious that she wants me to leave and never wants to lay eyes on me again. It will be the worst day of my life!
Alternative: I've been through lots of awkward situations and survived. (fact/true/helpful)

I can't stand it.
Alternative: At most it will be uncomfortable, but I will survive. (helpful)

When you concentrate on rational thinking, your subjective level of discomfort will drop from around 90% to maybe a 30-40% degree of discomfort.

This level is much easier to manage, and there will no longer be the irrational feelings of dread and fear. You can turn up to any such event, and you will be OK.

CHAPTER NINE

MORE HELPFUL STUFF

Thought records are a useful exercise and a great visual aid to how a rational approach can work systematically. But they are not something that you can do anywhere at any time. They are excellent to do at the end of each day, or as soon as you can after something perceptually awful has happened and you have become upset.

The following techniques, however, are a lot more mobile and much easier to grasp.

1. THE DE-CATASTROPHIZING SCALE

This technique provides a very quick way to de-catastrophize a situation.

Going back to the meeting-the-boyfriend's-mother scenario, our imaginary gf has wound herself up to 90 units of distress (SUDs). Not surprising with that thinking!

If the gf turned up in my office, I would say, "OK,

we're going to create a perspective scale." It would look a bit like the illustration on the next page.

I would ask her to imagine leaving my office and receiving a call to say that her parents have been involved in a near-fatal car crash.

> **Me:** "Where would you rate that on the scale?"
> **Gf:** "That would be over 100%."
> **Me:** "It has to be on the scale."
> **Gf:** "Well, in that case, it would be 100%."
> **Me:** "They're still alive."
> **Gf:** "OK, then, that would be 99%."
> **Me:** "So if we go back to the lunch with your boyfriend's mother, where would that be on the scale?"
> **Gf:** "I guess that would be a lot less, maybe only 40%."

As you can see, the fear of the lunch encounter and how bad that might feel has decreased by 50%. Just like magic. The scale has allowed things to be put into perspective, hence the decrease in the degree of distress.

CALM —— THINKING OF MEETING MOTHER —— MELTDOWN

The de-catastrophizing scale, also
known as the terribleness scale.

When something happens and you feel bad, or you feel bad in advance of a particular situation, the question you need to ask yourself is:

"In reality, how bad is this situation?"

You could write the question on a piece of card and keep it in your wallet, or type it into your phone, so that you can refer to it whenever you need to, reminding you to keep yourself grounded in reality.

Writing things like this down (or keying it into your phone) and keeping it with you is a powerful technique for de-catastrophizing. Also known as:

2. FLASH CARDS

Flash cards are a helpful set of "on the move" tools. You can write the beliefs you need to work out on small cards that you can carry in your purse or wallet, referring to them whenever you need to. Or, as mentioned, type them into your phone.

If you are concentrating on a way of thinking that you do over and over again, it will require attention to shift the habit. Look at that card three or four times a day, for at least fifteen seconds each time.

The fifteen seconds is recommended in the literature as it gives enough time for the brain to register the thought, not just look at it and then instantly discard it. You are trying to kindle new tracks in your brain. This way you will eventually access the rational with the same ease that you previously accessed the negative and irrational.

Here are some examples of flash cards you may find helpful. Feel free to add your own on the reverse sides—use anything you have found in the book that really resonated with you.

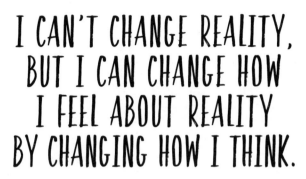

I CAN'T CHANGE REALITY,
BUT I CAN CHANGE HOW
I FEEL ABOUT REALITY
BY CHANGING HOW I THINK.

- - - - - - - - - - - - - - -

SOMETHING FALSE CAN
FEEL VERY TRUE. I MUSTN'T
LET A FEELING CONVINCE
ME IT'S A FACT.

- - - - - - - - - - - - - - -

THE WAY I THINK
CREATES HOW I FEEL.

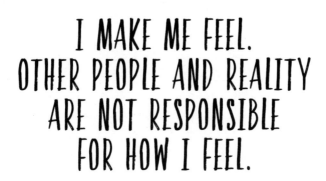

I MAKE ME FEEL.
OTHER PEOPLE AND REALITY
ARE NOT RESPONSIBLE
FOR HOW I FEEL.

- - - - - - - - - - - -

PERCEIVED THREATS ARE
NOT LIFE-THREATENING.

- - - - - - - - - - - -

WHERE IS THIS
THINKING TAKING ME?

HOW IS THIS THINKING
HELPING ME?

FEELINGS ARE NOT FACTS.
BELIEFS ARE NOT FACTS.

DISCOMFORT MAY BE
UNCOMFORTABLE,
BUT IT WON'T KILL ME.
JUST BREATHE
AND RIDE IT OUT.

FACT VS. OPINION

REAL VS. IDEAL

TRUE/HELPFUL

The last card, a simplified illustration of the matrix, is a helpful one to carry around to remind you how to check your thinking. Remember, *opinions and ideals are at the base of irrational thinking.*

- If someone has a negative opinion of you, that does not make it a fact. (fact versus opinion)
- If other people think you "should" be doing things a certain way, that is their ideal, not what your real world is about and not what is true. (real versus ideal)
- If someone says something negative about you and you can't get it out of your mind, is it helpful for you to continue visiting the thought? (true/helpful)

3. BREATHING

When you are feeling anxious, it can really help if you remember to breathe. That sounds a bit crazy because we're always breathing, right? But what happens when you're anxious is that you can tend to hold your breath, and this makes everything worse. When you feel like that, try this:

- Hold your breath for six counts (don't make the mistake of taking a deep breath)
- Breathe out
- Breathe in for three counts
- Breathe out for three counts
- Breathe in for three counts
- And so on . . .

The following app is on my Doctor Know Tumblr blog, and lots of people have found it really helpful: https://bit.ly/2TuiuvH

ONE MORE FROM THE TOOL KIT

A helpful checklist for challenging irrational thinking

Could I be . . .?

- mind reading?
- jumping to conclusions?
- assuming my view is the only possible one?
- paying attention only to the negative side of things?
- overestimating the chances of disaster?

- expecting myself or others to be perfect?
- totally condemning or labeling myself (or others) on the basis of a single event?
- using a double standard?
- worrying about how things *should* be instead of accepting and dealing with them as they are?
- thinking in all-or-nothing terms?
- using ultimatum words (must/should/have to) in my thinking?

CHAPTER TEN

WHICH TRACK WOULD YOU CHOOSE?

I had a few training sessions many years ago with a really nice guy who was a neurolinguistic programmer (an NLP works with the language of thought). He taught me the following metaphor.

Ready to do some imagining?

You have stopped on the side of the road on a grassy shoulder. On your left-hand side there is the track you always go down. It takes only minutes to get down it because the track is so well manicured. You don't slip, you don't slide; the track has little steps and even a little seat if you need to pause. All the shrubs are cut back so nothing gets caught up in your hair. No spiderwebs—they've all been cleared away. Not even any cockroaches.

Down you go like a kid on a waterslide, "Wheee!" and then you arrive at the bottom in front of a stinking open-air landfill. Seagulls floating above, scavenging and shitting everywhere, add to the summer stench.

It didn't take you long to get to your destination,

with all that ease of familiarity. But was it worth it? Doubt it!!

Back up on the grassy shoulder, on your right-hand side, there is another track. You don't go down that track very often, as it is quite awkward getting down it. You slip and slide and lose your footing, stuff gets caught up in your hair—there are cobwebs everywhere. Yuck! What an effort it is—so much more of a struggle than the other track. But when at last you get to the bottom . . . there is the most beautiful waterfall. You float in the water and feel contented and happy to be in your own skin.

EXPLAINING THE METAPHOR

OK, that was a metaphor for how the brain kindles thinking tracks. The point being, sure, you can go down the familiar track of negative thinking and end up feeling like shit: putting yourself down, doubting your ability, labeling yourself a loser. You can get there really fast and with minimal effort—but I don't believe that the advantage of speed outweighs the crap when you get there.

However, look at what happened when you chose the track less traveled. Of course, it took extra effort, but the reward was much greater. This track is obviously a metaphor for rational thinking. By choosing the more difficult path, you challenged your thinking habits and fought the irrational. Rational thinking gives you peace of mind. Think about that.

Choose your thoughts.
Challenge the bullshit!

Choose the thoughts
that take you to
the better outcome.

Choose the thoughts
that help you adapt.

CHAPTER ELEVEN

WINDING DOWN

"When you understand how you think,
you get to change how you feel."

Helping you achieve this was my goal when I wrote this book. Through my work and my personal experience of life, I understand the importance of feeling more in control and managing how you feel. When you achieve that, life is just that much easier. The answer lies in how you think about yourself in the world.

Of course, I have not been able to provide you with all the answers, but I hope I have given you enough of an understanding to make a difference. If you are still really struggling, I strongly suggest you seek help from a professional.

The world is always the same: it changes for better and for worse, but reality is always there. You get to better manage the unruly beast that is reality by managing the way you think. It is through this philosophy of thought that you will best be equipped.

Remember, life is full of the good and the bad, no matter who you are. Forget the word "deserve"—it does not apply. Otherwise, how do bad things happen to good people?

Sure, you don't get to change the world, but few people do. Most of us try to work within the realm of our own insignificance and be content with what we can contribute in the best way possible.

As psychoanalyst Anna Freud famously said: "If some longing goes unmet, don't be astonished. We call that Life."

It's OK not to change the world; it's OK to do what you can, when you can, and where you can. If what you achieve is a loving family, surrounded by lots of friends, helping people where you can, and eating good food, life would not be so bad, would it?

You don't need symbols of status—you don't need an expensive car or a designer wardrobe. Go for contentment: it really is the ultimate prize. The rest is just a bonus.

IN THE END

I can't possibly know what you might have taken from this book. I certainly hope that through the examination of thought you have learned how to manage your anxiety. The application of this knowledge is up to you in the end.

I empathize greatly with your struggles existing in this contemporary world. However, I want you to understand that so much of your discomfort or "disease" has to do with your perception of the world, not the reality of it.

I am hopeful that this book will enlighten you to the reality of the world, its injustice, its brutality, its uncaring nature, and, by the same token, its opportunities, beauty, and magnificence. I am hopeful that you will learn to adapt to whatever life throws at you, and that with the skills I have provided, you can enjoy and appreciate your one turn at being in Mother Nature's garden.

"Look DEEP into nature and you will understand everything better."

—Albert Einstein

GREAT MINDS THAT I HAVE QUOTED

- Dr. Aaron Beck
- Dr. David Burns
- Charles Darwin
- Albert Einstein
- Albert Ellis
- Anna Freud
- Theodore Roosevelt
- Hans Selye
- William Shakespeare
- Socrates

GLOSSARY

all-or-nothing thinking: Also known as black-and-white thinking. Imagining something is either extremely good or extremely bad. No middle ground.

amygdala: Part of the brain that is involved in processing emotions.

anxiety: General term for feelings of worry, fear or panic, usually in anticipation of a particular event.

black-and-white thinking, *see* **all-or-nothing thinking**

catastrophizing: Regarding or describing a situation as being much worse than it actually is.

cognitive behavioral therapy (CBT): Type of psychotherapy that involves addressing negative or irrational thought patterns or behavioral habits and replacing them with a realistic, positive approach.

cognitive distortions: Patterns of thought that are irrational and unhelpful.

cognitive restructuring: The process of learning to identify the negative or irrational thoughts as they appear.

cognitive theory: A way of explaining how your thought processes influence your behavior.

depression: An illness characterized by sadness and loss of interest in things you usually enjoy.

emotional reasoning: Deciding something is true based on an emotional reaction rather than fact.

epigenetics: The study of "nature versus nurture," or how you are affected by factors other than your gene sequence—for example, diet, aging, or family environment.

fortune telling: In a psychological context, fortune telling is the act of predicting a negative outcome, regardless of its likelihood.

magnification, *see* **catastrophizing**

mind reading: Assuming that we know what other people are thinking without any discussion or evidence.

minimization: Regarding or describing a situation as being of much lower significance than it actually is.

negative automatic thinking: Negative thoughts that occur spontaneously in everyday life.

negative mental filter: Focusing only on the negative possibilities of a situation.

overgeneralizing: Applying one prospective outcome to all future situations and/or imagining a far-fetched conclusion (e.g., "My life is over"; "I can't cope with this").

perceptual filter: A way of perceiving the world that is distorted by your feelings or beliefs.

personalization: Blaming yourself unfairly for a negative occurrence.

social anxiety: A condition characterized by an irrational fear of being negatively evaluated (judged) by other people.

strain: Physical or emotional pressure or force.

subjective units of distress (SUDs): A scale for measuring the degree of stress experienced by an individual.

thought viruses, *see* **cognitive distortions**

AUTHOR PHOTOGRAPH BY DAVID K. SHIELDS

ABOUT THE AUTHOR

Gwendoline Smith, B.Soc.Sci., M.Soc.Sci. (Hons.), Dip.Clin.Psych., is a clinical psychologist, speaker, blogger, and the author of the books *Depression Explained* and *Sharing the Load*, among others. She also goes by the name Doctor Know.

Andrews McMeel Publishing
a division of Andrews McMeel Universal
1130 Walnut Street, Kansas City, Missouri 64106

www.andrewsmcmeel.com

First published in 2017; revised edition published in 2019 by Allen & Unwin NZ (New Zealand).

20 21 22 23 24 BVG 10 9 8 7 6 5 4 3 2 1

ISBN: 978-1-5248-6045-5

Library of Congress Control Number: 2020931559

Editor: Allison Adler
Art Director: Spencer Williams
Production Editor: Elizabeth A. Garcia
Production Manager: Carol Coe

ATTENTION: SCHOOLS AND BUSINESSES
Andrews McMeel books are available at quantity discounts with bulk purchase for educational, business, or sales promotional use. For information, please e-mail the Andrews McMeel Publishing Special Sales Department: specialsales@amuniversal.com.

Listen up! Enjoy *The Book of Knowing* in audio, available wherever audiobooks are sold.